Wednesday's Writer

12

The Epitome of a Twelfth Anthology from the Todmorden Writers' Group

December 2021

Compiled by Andy Fraser, Theresa Sowerby & Zoë Collins

Edited by Andy Fraser & Zoë Collins

Contents

Introduction

This year has been one of hope and loss. It began with a second lockdown throughout the UK which, if possible, affected us all more than the first in 2020. During this time, the Wednesday Writers were confined to attending meetings on Zoom. This was tolerable but we yearned for more - to meet and chat face-to-face, to sit in a real room with real people, rather than heads in virtual boxes. However, one of the inspirations during this time was the flourishing of our online open mic evenings. New friends from across the world joined us for a beautiful coming-together of cultures and viewpoints in a safe and supportive environment. We owe all of the participants a huge thank you for keeping us happy and sane through those long, dark months. To this end, we have included a special section in this year's anthology dedicated to our wonderful online community. With the help of the Todmorden Writers' Collective (TWC), we hope to purchase equipment that will enable us to further these ties, hosting live and online hybrid open mic events in the future.

In 2021 we also lost a wonderful member of the group. Glenys Halliday had been with the Wednesdays for only a year, but her poems, filled with wit and the deepest humanity, always made us laugh, even during the peak of Covid-19. For this reason, we have included a couple of poems from Glenys in her absence. She is sorely missed.

Recently, the world changed for the better. People now walk the streets once more, fill the cafés, bars and restaurants, and we are able to meet face-to-masked face once again. While the threat of another lockdown is ever-present, the Wednesday Writers are currently back where we belong, in our spiritual home at the Honest John. We have begun to host the TWC open mic nights live in the Golden Lion, as well as online. It is a joy and a relief to be together again after so long apart.

With all the negativity of the last year, you would imagine the pieces of writing created during this time would be glum and introspective. Not a bit of it. As always, the Wednesday Writers approach each challenge with a variety of styles, points of view and imagination that continues to amaze. In this anthology you will find everything from poems of love and loss to stories that both ground us and take us out of this world.

If you have a passion for writing, whether as a hobby or a profession, and would like further information on the Wednesday Writers, please drop us an email at todwedwriters@outlook.com and I'll be happy to let you know more.

Andy Fraser
Chair of the Wednesday Writers
November 2021

Desire Lines

Desire Lines
by *Gina Perry*

A whim took me along a knotted path through a clover field,
Over a rotting style
Into a meadow
Of wildflowers.
Upon flattened ground
I ambled on
Through walls of grass
On an invisible path
That weaved through gaps in hedgerows
Between fence posts
Over stepping-stones
And into the distance
To follow the lines sewn across the landscapes.
Trod by cattle and cart
and foot leads a trail
Formed by itself
From a yearning to walk on
Following the desire
To know what's on the other side.

Nyctophobic Kate

Nyctophobic Kate
by *Richard Holley*

Nyctophobic Kate shifted down the pothole whilst the rest of the team waited at the entrance; she insisted on going alone. I will face my fears Mark, it's what you wanted, I owe you this, I can move, I can breathe. There will be light like the green of the trees, like Christmas and that holiday staying in some old house in the Alps. Like the red of her dress and golden hair, like playing in the autumn leaves after school.

'That really narrows it down.'

'She's a princess, I think, but there's something wrong.'

'You're telling me there's something wrong.'

'Don't laugh Mark, it's important to me.'

'I'm sorry I just don't get living in the past, when all it does is make you feel bad.'

'I just want to find that book.'

Kate's memories always became more vivid in moments of heightened stress, it was how she dealt with fear and sadness; particularly utilised was her earliest and most peaceful childhood memory of a book, the pictures at least; she couldn't remember the title.

I should never have accused you of not caring, when you spent so many hours trudging round all those second-hand and rare bookshops, always trying to feel a rare interest.

Kate pulled out of the tight-throated passage into a chamber in which she could reach out with gloved hands at nothing more than a ghostly emptiness. She raised her head, gingerly despite the protective helmet. Not limited by any roof, she got to her knees and switched on her torch. She passed the beam over the silver-streaked rocks, then stood up in the whispering dark, whispering that broke into a roar as stones rumbled in the gasping passage by which she had entered the now inescapable underworld.

You must be here Mark. I'd be scared if I was truly alone, and I don't feel scared. Good idea though for me to face my fears, I'm no longer scared of being trapped, I'm just actually trapped.

'I might not always be there for you, you know.'

I wonder if you knew right then that you were dying; some people have an inkling. That twinkling still there in your eyes, swimming amongst the murk of morphine, gave you crazy ideas, like when you said I should face my nyctophobia on my own. Not your last wish though, not the last thing you said to me. My protector, then my guide on how to protect myself. You found me at what was then the darkest point in my life, though this literally is now the darkest point in my life. Are you here? I shouldn't have nagged you so much about that book. You'd always been more interested in exploring real life forests than reading about them in books.

'As well as finding my own real-life princess.'

Always the charmer. You made me feel like I could do anything, that's why I'm not scared.

With sound as her only guide, Kate slowly explored her uncharted surroundings, drawn by the hollow echo of the water of the depths, a tiny splinter off the river Styx. Amongst those echoes she made out the sound of human voices, not Mark's but then she remembered Mark's from those last days in hospital.

'I never did find that book for you, I wish I had done.'

'It was a distorted childhood memory, I probably found it loads of times and just didn't realise.'

'No, you would've known. I wish I'd found it.'

The last thing you ever said to me. I shouldn't have caused that to be your dying wish.

Kate's memory had become so vivid as to almost overlap into her consciousness of the sensory deprivation of the cave.

There must be an opening to above ground, she thought, and following the dim chorus of overland planning and fretting began to perceive a faint glimmer of light from a singular shaft. Merging with the solitary luminescence she looked up and was about to call out when her foot touched something that slid over the mossy stone and that she instinctively knew had no business existing right then and there but for the end of days.

She looked down to where the light as from Arthurian legend illuminated not a sword in the stone but a book atop stone, and not just any book but 'the' book.

'Sir Gawain and the Loathly Lady! You found it for me! Mark! You're here! I know you must be here!'

'Kate.'

Kate flashed the torch around as if the dark could be cleaned away from a cave any easier than dirt.

'Don't be scared.'

'I'm not scared, let me see you.'

'You can't.'

'Please let me see you.'

'I'm here with you, but you can't see me; this was my last wish.'

'Won't you stay?'

'This was my unfinished business; it's time to let go, you've got the rest of your life to live and you don't need me now.'

'I will always need you.'

'And I'll be waiting.'

It was hours before the potholing team dug through to the cave, though they worked with the speed of desperation to save a life. It was therefore all the more bizarre for them to find Kate reading under what seemed like a heaven-sent shaft of light, with a look of uncanny childlike contentment in her face.

Shadow

Shadow
by *Theresa Sowerby*

It's there in the left hand corner
behind Father, as he stands
in his Air Force uniform
(the photo black and white,
fading a little to brown),

the shadow, not thrown
by light, which followed him,
stretched beside him at night.
When you first noticed it,
asked Mother what it was,

she said, There's nothing there,
only the photographer's white cloth.
But when he sat you on his knee,
you felt its weight
drawing you earthwards.

He has no grave, his plane
gone down in the Pacific. Only you
know the gravity
that drew him, even as he flew,
whispering, Let go.

Now you take out
your son's school photo –
Luke's smile, black curls – and see,
forming behind his left shoulder,
a gathering of grey.

Red as Snow

Red as Snow
by *Iain Mackness*

I wander along the road, my boots crunching the untouched flurry of snow. A sound unlike any other, except perhaps the rubbing of cotton wool.

As far as I can see there are snow-capped peaks. A generous icing sugar shake on each. The words of that song from the film *Frozen* flash through my head. And I realise once again that I've got them wrong. Memory is such a fragile thing.

Inevitably my mind wanders. I can feel it trying to access something long buried. Something hard.

Instead, I recall winters past when my mum would come into my room early and tell me to look outside. Seeing the garden transformed into a magical Narnia. How I'd dress in the shortest time possible, run downstairs, grab my mittens and duffle coat and dash outside, hampered only by my mum putting plastic bags over my hands so my gloves wouldn't get soaked. Not having enough snow to build my own snowman, and using an upturned bin as the body. Wondering if a snow Dalek would work better.

The snowball catches me square in the face. I hadn't even noticed the kids walking nearby, parents somewhere distant. I wipe the already melting projectile from my bruised cheek and glare at my assailants.

'Sorry!' one of them shouts out, seemingly in earnest. At least they're polite delinquents. It seems as if I was not the intended target.

'No problem,' I say, secretly wanting to pelt them back with even bigger and denser snowballs.

And then the memory hits me. With a force much greater than my recent assault.

I'm ten and walking up a hill with my best friend. It's winter and we are off school for Christmas. I'm wearing proper gloves and no longer have to add plastic bags on top. Trees crowd together around us, and there's a constant sprinkling of water droplets from the branches overhead. The trail we are on has been well trodden and there is more mud now than snow beneath our wellies.

But as we move further along we see a clearing, untouched. A canopy of trees protects the white treasure beneath. We rush towards it. Matthew gets there first, effortlessly picking up a handful of snow and throwing it my way. He's a bad shot, but I duck – in the process also getting ammunition. My throw is much truer and it hits him squarely in the chest. His Parka protects him, but there's some spray into his face.

He reloads, and this time I nearly get a snowball in the eye. Quick reflexes make me turn my head, and my hair cushions the blow slightly. I'm excited and slightly annoyed as I grab another handful of snow. For a split second I think I can feel something else, but the ball has already left my hand.

I felt something hard. I'm sure I felt something...

The shot hits home, right in Matthew's slightly pudgy face. I see him lose his footing, a comical dance as he tries to remain on his feet, then a fall back into the snow. I start to laugh...

But then I see a dark patch begin to spread from his head, a red stain infecting the once pristine snow behind him. I move closer and see that he isn't moving. The blood melts the ice immediately around his head, forming a red halo.

Time seems to stand still. I can't move or speak. There's only his head and the slowly expanding crimson stain.

But one other thing is clear. In the remains of my last snowball, a small stone. Black, and hard.

A Legacy

A Legacy
by *Shura Price*

The earth is warm,
welcoming weeds and my lettuce seeds;
his fork in my hand riddles the ground.
Cuticles laced with crescents of dirt,
my fingers, his fingers,
grip the familiar comfort of smooth wood
moulded to his palm, now mine.

And he is here:

in the scent of marigold leaves,
I see him planting my cherry tree,
leaving me a living legacy;
his eyes crinkle in a smile, one
underlined by a sickle shaped scar,
blue, a coal dust tattoo.

And he is here:

in the peony's lush white bloom.
Don't dig it in too deep, he'd said,
but the roots do need room to spread.
Underground his veined hands had hacked
at the bright black rock; at home nurtured
roses pink, scarlet and one called blue moon.

When the earth is warm, and bluebells paint the
shadows I picture the jam jar with the sunflower
yellow lid that father and I hid in his shed;
the shaky letters on the label said:
'soil from Ukraine cherry tree garden'.
At his funeral we crumbled the earth
from his homeland over his coffin.

In my pantry where I store the preserves,
is a screw-top jar,
empty so far.

Inner Animal

Inner Animal
by *Dave Badrick*

Hmmm, nice warm furry bodies, sniffling, snoring and shuffling around together. Someone sucking noisily on a teat, someone yawning. Hmmm, maybe I'm hungry too ...

Screech! Clang! The jarring noise of a bolt being opened jolted Sam out of his reverie. The cosiness of his dream was crushed by the mixture of hope and trepidation that accompanied any human activity in the compound. He could hear and smell the New Boss, and that increased his levels of agitation; and he could feel his bladder tighten as he warily got up from his bed and tried to peer through the wire mesh in his pen door. He couldn't see anything interesting – just the same old corridor wall with his lead hanging down off a hook. The New Boss's footsteps approached, and other footsteps and voices increased his anxiety and he peed a bit on the doorpost to relieve the tightness. *Maybe if I make a noise they'll notice me* he thought as he jumped up and scrambled with his front legs on the door mesh.

The New Boss made angry noises at him as he walked past. A small pack of humans followed – two adults and a pup carrying a stick – and they disappeared out of his sight. He could hear that they'd stopped further along the corridor and he became aware of a faint tapping of the stick on the metal grille of the pens. Something triggered an angry reflex; he got noisier. The vague memory of a group of human pups every morning and evening - jeering, throwing stones and noisily slapping chain link fencing with sticks. The hair on his back bristled and the scars on his neck felt sore where the chain collar had tightened and restrained his frantic efforts to get at those pups.

Sam quietened as soft, cooing sounds drifted along the corridor from the visiting pack, and Sam felt jealous of whoever was getting the attention. After a few minutes he could hear them coming back, and just as he jumped up on the door, the pup human appeared. The pup squealed and then howled as he ran to the bitch human and Sam could smell blood and see it dripping from a cut on the pup's hand. The New Boss made really angry noises and uncomprehendingly Sam slunk into a corner of his pen. The New Boss had never beaten him like the Old Boss had, but Sam's reflex was to cower in subordination. He licked his sore claw where he'd raked it down the sharp ends of the wire grille and got a strange metallic human taste.

Sam felt lonely, insecure and miserable. Over the next few days the New Boss and his pack of humans made disapproving noises while they fed him and cleaned the runny shit which seeped out of him. They took him for brief walks but put a nasty scratchy muzzle on him, tightened his collar so he could hardly produce a wheezy bark, and pulled impatiently on a short tight lead. No gentle noises for him.

Although it was boring and uneventful, after a while the routine soothed Sam's nervousness. One morning he heard the sound of visitors and his heart sank as he recognised the whiny voice of that pup human. His bowels hurt, and he whined and let out a smelly fart just as his view of the outside world was suddenly and noisily blanked out by a big wooden board across his door.

Disconcerted and despite his desperation not to get agitated, his instinct kicked in when the human footsteps went past, and he leapt uncontrollably at the covered door, snarling and slavering. More harsh raised noises from the New Boss. Eventually he tired and quietened and became forlornly aware of those soft, comforting noises again. The humans came back but this time Sam could hear the soft scratching of canine claws and smelt the pungent but freshly soaped fur of that big, old, ugly bitch from down the corridor.

Sam realised that this had become a familiar scenario – the six or seven dogs that he'd seen or heard on the day he'd first arrived had all been visited and then left as part of a new human pack. Screech! Clang! His bladder tightened but his anxiety became tinged with hope as he heard and then smelt humans ... maybe he was being visited ... maybe it was his turn.

Yes! The New Boss was making low, comforting noises as he opened the pen and the humans entered. Sam stood quiet but pensive. Just the New Boss and another unfamiliar adult human. Not much of a pack but better than this spirit-sapping loneliness. Sam lay down passively, soothed by more soft, gentle murmurs. Oh! A sharp scratch on the back of his neck. Drowsiness, the smell of piss and a nice warm feeling in his groin as he snuggled up to the white-coated human. Hungry. Where's that teat! Ummm!

Milk and Water Stockings

Milk and Water Stockings
by *Laura Barnes*

Let 'em play, God knows
They'll be sweating cotton before they can count
Let them coax their little fires
It's just old useless tat and a single clog
Spitting, smoking, blazing in the terraces
Since Alice Southwell went missing

And the drinking men laughing down their pints
Pulling faces of a girl weak in intellect
Strong as a ram and dark of skin
The women whispering
Poor wretch in her milk and water stockings
And her brown stuff dress
Oh such high cut hair

The farm boys, last to see her
Knew her to be trusting
As playful as a puppy dog
But she didn't return their calling
Walking sore footed over Rochdale moors
Her petticoat laid over her arm.

The Distance Between Us

The Distance Between Us
by *Andy Fraser*

'I can see it so clear. I'll get out the cab and it'll be a clear, fall morning, you know? An Oregon Special, all crisp an' gold with a chill in the air you can almost smell, right? Almost taste it on your tongue.' The intercom crackles through the darkness.

'Right. I'm there with you, buddy.'

'I'll walk up to that old house, flake off some of the rusting paintwork round the door. I been meaning to do it for years. I'll open the fly-screen and hammer on that door 'til someone comes to see what the hullabaloo's about.' A snatched laugh is followed by a lengthier cough. Over the comms, the sigh and pop of the respirators stay constant.

'My wife'll most likely answer the door and she'll be all fiery, shouting "What's with all the noise" and – You remember my wife, Roger?'

'Janice? Yeah, I remember Janice. A peach.'

'Yeah, Janice is a peach all right. And she'll come out all angry thinking it's kids playing up and then she'll see me standing there and she'll shut her mouth and not say a word. Not a damn word. She'll put her hands over her mouth so she don't think I can see her crying, but her eyes'll be full of tears. So, I'll hold her, an' I'll kiss them tears from her cheeks and that salt'll taste so sweet an' warm, and I'll breathe her in. I'll breathe in her body like it was damn perfume. You remember the perfume, Roger? I used to put it on my pillow, to remind me of her. Yeah, I'll lose myself in that perfume.'

'Sounds perfect, Paul.'

'And the kids'll come out, screaming and I'll pick them up, all of them together, one in each hand an' one climbing on my back, and they'll be laughing an' a-hollering, 'Daddy! Daddy!' and Janice'll be crying an' kissing my face and, and all a sudden, I'll catch pot-roast in my nostrils and it'll stop me dead. Yeah, Janice's pot-roast. I can almost taste it now.'

'Bit of luck and you'll be tucking into it in no time.'

'Yeah. Right...'

The respirators thump like pistons, then pause before the long sigh of air gets sucked into their suits. They don't speak. The intercom crackles with interference, then the respirators pop once more.

'Okay Roger, you better do it.'

'You sure, buddy?'

'Yeah, I'm sure. We've wasted enough time already.'

'Okay. Here goes.'

Roger presses a button on the dark console before him. The light from his helmet is just sufficient to see Paul, crouched in the centre of a circular cradle; the bulk of his environment suit shrinks him, like a kid in adult clothes. They look at each other for a few moments, then a surge in power and an arcing lattice of light surrounds Paul, bouncing off his body, causing it to convulse and spasm. It penetrates deep into his suit, his flesh, his mind, absorbing and irradiating.

Then it's over. The broken Med bay of the *Elysium* falls into darkness once more. There is a tense silence.

'That it?' Paul gasps eventually.

'Guess so,' Roger replies. 'How'd it feel?'

'Thought it would hurt more.'

'Yeah? Looked like it hurt.'

'Nah. Not so's I remember.' Paul's breathing, even enhanced by the respirator, is noticeably weaker. 'Freaky though.'

'Good to know.'

'Okay, your turn.'

**

They might never find out what caused the explosion that ripped through the oxygen tanks. Paul and Roger had been working in the aquaponics dome when they saw the fireball. It engulfed the Hab unit in brilliant, bright flame without any heat or sound. They ran as fast as their suits and Mars' gravity allowed, but without atmosphere the flames died instantly. As they got closer, their fear increased. Lab and Control were nothing more than blackened stubs where walls had once been. The skin, that kept the planet out and the air in, was gone. The Hab unit was missing its roof. It dawned on both men that those inside would not have had time to reach their suits before exposure took them.

Paul collapsed to his knees, Roger yelled names over the comms, but only their laboured breathing came back to them. Then the Hab door opened. One of the younger scientists, Lisette maybe, staggered out. The oxygen in her suit burned bright yellow as she tried to remove her helmet. When they reached her, she was already frozen, her eyes filled red with blood, staring into the next life.

They spent two hours checking charred remains against nametags and thanked Heaven they couldn't smell anything. Finally, they concluded that they were the only survivors. Even if the *Elysium* could be repaired, neither of them could pilot her.

***

Paul unplugs his suit from the cradle and makes his way to the console while Roger staggers ungracefully toward the cradle. Their suits get in the way, the depleted oxygen mix in their helmets makes them giddy. They fall over like drunkards. A fall that is noticeably slower than on Earth.

'How long?' Roger asks, shaking a device on his wrist.

'I make it seven minutes.'

'Damn, so do I.'

Paul is now crawling along the floor. Open to the elements, dust settles everywhere; on the kit, on the consoles, on the shapes that he still recognises as colleagues. The respirators continue their long hiss and short pop. It is all there is now. Their suits leave senses only as memories, imagined. Paul clings to the hiss and pop, the wheeze and thump until he finds the teleport console.

'What about you?' he asks.

'What about me?' Roger plugs his suit into the cradle's web of tubes. 'When I get back, you mean?'

'Yeah. You got anyone waiting for you?'

'I'll probably go see my Mom. Dad died three years back and she ain't been so good, neither.'

'Sorry to hear that, man.' Paul watches from behind the console. The single active button gives off a pale red light - charging.

'Yeah, well, we weren't real close ... To tell the truth, I think I might have come out here just to get away from her, get away from...' A sound that might be a cough or might be a sigh. 'Anyways, it's the place I'd go back to. It's home, you know? Maybe I'll take round a plate of them French profiteroles, Mom always likes a profiterole.'

'Yeah? Who doesn't?' Paul notices his glove is shaking in the helmet torchlight but the button is large. He just needs to wait, calm, breathe. 'So, where's your Mom live?'

'One of the rambling old Colonial pads, just outside Belle Chasse.'

'New Orleans?'

'Yeah, that's it, the old town. You ever been?'

'Nah, Portland boy. Louisiana's the other side of the world.' Paul's breathing is sounding shallow as a puddle.

'Pity. It's beautiful down there this time of year.' There is a sigh over the intercom that is not part of the respirator cycle. 'Jazz Festival be on round about now. You like jazz, Paul?'

'Not my kind of –' Coughing cuts off any explanation.

The two men stand in silence, talk now a luxury. The button on the console finally turns green.

'Ready when you are,' Paul whispers.

'I'm ready.' Roger's voice breaks. 'Hit that button, buddy.'

'Bon voyage,' Paul controls his thick glove, pressing down on the pulsing green light. Blue electrics dance around the cradle. Light arcs and snatches at Roger's body. It slices through suit and man forcing his muscles to spasm. Roger cries out and Paul cries with him, with the memory. When it is over, he lets himself slide down the front of the console, onto the hard reality of the ground. He imagines Roger doing the same, lying on his back looking at the stars through the *Elysium's* devastated hull. Maybe he is looking at the same faint blue light that could, if you believed hard enough, be Earth.

The intercom crackles. 'How long now?'

Paul is slow to respond; his brain feels two metres behind his body. He raises his arm to look at the oxygen gauge, but his eyes no longer focus. 'Don't know. How long you think we got?'

'Three minutes?'

'Sounds about right.'

Another silence blows across the darkness, only the sweep and drop of their respirators for company. The air mixed thinner and thinner with each breath.

'Before he died, my dad told me souls were lighter than air.'

'You figure?'

'He said that way they float up to heaven when you die. Like when you burn pages of the bible.'

'You burned bibles?'

'Well yeah, the free ones. The pages are so thin, when they burn you can watch them float away 'til pouf, they're gone.'

'You.' Paul breath now catches in his throat. 'Irreligious. Son-of-a. Bitch.'

Roger smiles. He turns his head so he is looking out to the Hab units he helped build. To the blackened walls, the ruptured hull, the asphyxiated body in the doorway. They lie this way for a time. Thinking, just thinking.

'How long 'til we get home?'

'Six. minutes.' Paul's response is immediate.

'Means we're going to be dead three and a half minutes before we get home.'

'Don't go there...'

'You don't think it's strange? We're going to die here while those creepy-ass bodies...'

'You read. the insurance.'

'Yeah, but still. If we're here, how can they be us?'

'Who the hell. else would. they be?'

'Damn imposters, that's who they'll be. Look like us, talk like us, smell and taste. Remember all the things we remember. Nobody's even going to know we died.'

'That's. the point. We won't.' Paul's whisper is barely audible. 'We'll be... alive.' His respirator makes one final gasp of air and to his mind it smells of pot-roast.

Roger notices only one pop and wheeze now. Suddenly, it is important to talk, to cover the silence, the absence. 'Hey buddy. Guess we don't. get to do. the Oates thing, huh? No "I'm just. going outside...". We're already there. ain't nothing but dust.' A tear makes his vision swim as his respirator slows and sighs its last. 'They never. found Oates. neither.'

Roger gazes up into the sky, black and speckled with lights. They glitter and flare like tiny flames, floating ever-upward and there in the middle is a faint blue light that could, if he believed hard enough, be Heaven.

Lone Shoe

Lone Shoe
by *Karla Butler*

We were poor, hand to mouth. Each morning we woke up cold and hungry, wondering what we could scavenge from the bins. Passers-by would spit at us. Sometimes on a night they would throw food at us and scream, Get a job. Like we wanted to live like this.

Danny was different to me. Every day I woke up and felt that I didn't want to live anymore. What was the point of it? Each breath I took I was reminded of how much I've failed. But when I looked at Danny he would brighten my day, just for being Danny. He always made me laugh with stories of parties he'd been to, celebrities he'd slept with. Leonardo DiCaprio was his favourite. We saw Titanic three times. The manager would let us in for sneaky favours from Danny. I knew they were lies but he told them so well, I didn't care.

The nights were getting longer and the cold was getting to us now. Danny took desperate measures to make sure we had food in our bellies. Men would come by, old business types. He looked young enough to them. He'd lie about his age. We were 24, but we didn't look it. He'd say he was 17 and they lapped it up. At first it was small things, hand jobs here and there, then it would get more serious. He'd go for days with these men. He'd come back with his face bashed up. My Danny was disappearing. He no longer told stories, he was silent as we ate the food – the bad taste of our KFC he bought with the money he was given. He wouldn't stop though I begged him. I knew one day he would not come back, either in mind or body. One day that did happen. The night before, a very expensive car pulled up, an elderly man was sat in the back seat and the driver told Danny to get in the car. I begged him not to, but he did it anyway. I searched the streets for days, weeks. When I went to the police station they just laughed at me.

In time I managed to get off the streets and made a life for myself. I never completely forgot about Danny , I just tried to move on with my life.

I don't know why I chose to change my route to work today, but I felt compelled to check our old haunt – perhaps it was an old song on the radio. I spotted an Adidas Samba trainer, bright blue, along the side of the path where we spent our nights begging. But why now? It's been 20 years since we saw each other. I picked up the shoe. Why would I find this now? Was it Danny's? How could it be? Finding it here near the boarded up cafe, where we'd slept many years ago. There was quite few of us along the street, with our made up shelter, we were stronger together, we all protected each other. I don't know why but I always felt I had a duty to Danny so I've decided to rent a flat nearby, just in case I see him again.

Lone Shoe *was first published in Crown and Pen Zine, June 2021.*

Curiosity

Curiosity
by *Hannah Godden*

I had his heart for a while,
turned it over in my hands
to feel its sticky weight,
pressed it with finger and thumb
to check for blocked valves,
leaks, tissue damage,
scraped off some dirt
from its warmth with a fingernail.

I had his heart for a while,
held it to my nose
and sniffed its sickly tang
of iron and rust
(not rotten but wouldn't
keep it in my pocket),
tested it with a quick flick
of the tongue, coppery
but bland like unsalted soup.

I had his heart for a while,
took it in my mouth like a cat
with a shrew, gently gently
carried through kitchen
and lounge, then pricked
with tooth and claw,
'til it ran with a squeal
beneath floorboards
and out the cellar door.

The Mirror

The Mirror
by *Steve Welsh*

'My daughter was buried when she was thirteen,' he said.

'That must have been difficult,' I said.

'Poor girl didn't see it coming.'

'And your wife? You said your wife died soon after?'

'Two months after. She was never going to get over our daughter's death.'

'Well, that figures, I suppose. Now then, just a second,' I said, 'If you could stand with your back to the wooden post.'

'Like this?'

'That's fine. Now, put your hands behind the post. That's right. I'll tie them together.'

'I understand.'

'Tell me then. I'm interested. Your daughter? She was the first person you killed?'

'That's right. Then my wife. Then all the others.'

'But not your son?'

'Only women. It's always been women. My son left home soon after. I've no idea where he is.'

'I'm interested though. What got you started? I mean, most people take up hobbies.'

'I can tell you exactly when I started. I was ten and I was playing with my pet rabbit in the garden. At the bottom of our drive there was a grey squirrel and I watched it jumping across the road. Then along came a motorbike and went right over it. It curled into a ball and as the motorbike drove off, it relaxed out of the ball and lay still on the road. All of a sudden, like a blinding revelation, I realised that there's such a difference between a dead body and a living body. So then I started to

41

strangle the rabbit and I watched its eyes as the life went out of it. I found it, well, I found it, what can I say, I found it exciting.'

'Exciting? Do you mean what I think you mean?'

'You of all people, I think, will understand me. Yes. I get aroused. Having a women's life in my hands, it sort of turns me on. Do you know what I mean?'

'Not really. For me, it's all about money. Your daughter? Your wife? All the women? You strangled them all?'

'I've never thought of any other method. I can feel the warmth of their bodies. I can see into their eyes. It's their eyes that get me. One moment, sparkling with life. Then, glazed over. It's that change when life becomes death. And it's me. It's me making that change for them.'

'So that's why you want this mirror?'

'Exactly. You've positioned it perfectly. I can look into my own eyes.'

I passed a piece of rope around his neck and tied it into a knot behind the post. Then I inserted a two foot metal rod through the knot and turned it a couple of inches. Just enough to tighten it around his neck.

'Are you ready?' I said.

He looked into the mirror. I could see his reflection in it. There was a hint of a smile and his eyes seemed eager. Not like anyone else's I'd ever killed.

'I'll start turning the garrotte. But tell me, you haven't seen your son in a long time?'

'No. Why do you ask?'

'Because he's also given me money.'

'What do you mean? Why?'

I pulled out my stiletto and flicked it open.

'For two reasons. Firstly. You're certainly not going to get aroused by watching yourself in the mirror.'

I pulled his trousers down. Then his underpants.

'And you certainly won't be able to watch yourself in the mirror.'

I lifted the blade next to his eyes.

'Like I said, for me it's just about the money.'

I tightened the garrotte, but only to stop his screams. Then I got to work.

Putting the Record Straight

Putting the Record Straight
by *Deborah Lowe*

As this opportunity has presented itself I might as well make use of it to set things straight. I could let it lie, but no, I've got to worry at it till it's right, till the truth is known. We terriers are like that. I know we're famous for our skills as ratters, diggers, tenacious chasers of rabbits and so forth. But even though my own career has been, let us say, a little out of the common way for my sort, I've pursued it with the zeal and purpose of the first great elder terrier at that very first rabbit hole.

I am an artist's model and muse. I know, I know what you're thinking. I'm no leggy Irish wolfhound. You can't imagine me as the romantic hero, my head on the knee of a dying chieftain in a kilt. Those fancy sorts are all wrong for it in my opinion. But short as I am, I have had my moments. In fact I was the inspiration, you could say the figurehead, for the dawn of our modern age.

It's all in the training. My painter was a good sort. He'd picked up the commands for 'walk', and 'dinner' readily enough and I taught him a few rudimentary games with balls and sticks. He was a little oversensitive if I ate his yellow paint or chewed a brush, but you can't have everything.

What he really excelled at though was the Modelling game, basically a variant of 'sit-stay-fetch'. I taught him to lay out the tasty morsel. I'd model, he'd draw, then when I felt like he needed a break I'd snaffle it and we'd start over. We'd play the game till I was ready for my walk. No end of cold breakfast sausages I got out of that game. We'd ring the changes too, use props from around the studio, and it's this that brings me to heart of the matter.

That one portrait, or rather the title for it. Let me state for the record, there is no way any self-respecting dog would be fooled by that. We have first rate hearing, better than any human. It was a tempting little slice of pork pie in that trumpet contraption, not 'His master's voice!' The very idea!

Yours truly

Nipper Barraud

Epilogue:

The human opened the flap of the dusty cardboard box and lifted out a black wax cylinder, He fitted it carefully into the mahogany box of the gramophone and turned the handle. At first there was no sound other than a dry hissing, he leaned his head closer in to the brass trumpet, listening hard. Faintly at first, then increasing in volume emerged the annoyed barking of a small dog.

Hector's Thumb

Hector's Thumb
by *Theresa Sowerby*

The door closed.

Alysoun knelt before the open chest. From the folds of a shift, her hand withdrew a small book. She went to the bed, felt for the opening in its cover and slipped the volume into a gap in the straw, carefully re-weaving the strands so that it was concealed.

She sat down on the mattress and eased off her shoes and stockings. Her left foot twisted inwards. She rubbed it between her hands.

She could not be more than twelve, maybe thirteen years old, with an oval face and large dark eyes that shone too brightly.

The coarse cloth of her postulant's dress was rough against her neck and arms. A smell of piss mixed with lavender came from the garderobe in the closeted area behind the wall at her head.

She had some hours before she would be required in the refectory and had been excused service on this, her first afternoon. Tears stalled behind her eyes and she observed her white-clad body on the pallet as though it belonged to someone else.

Her thoughts felt dulled, as if wrapped in hessian. Were the outer walls – the tall stone walls that they had driven past to the solid wooden gate, as high as the walls – were these to be replicated in her mind, the one place she had thought to be free?

***

Sir Robert retired early to a small private room. The bed felt soft after hours of being thrown against the sides of the carriage. His mind dwelt on his daughter, left now to her life in the convent. Alysoun with her crippled foot and sharp mind. His Blackbird, as he had always called her. Had he done the right thing?

Hector's Thumb – the phrase came to him as he lay down.

Yes, it had been one late afternoon in the solar, he in his chair reading, Alysoun lying on the floor at his feet with his favourite greyhound. Idly running her finger down the dog's front leg, she had become suddenly attentive. When he looked up he saw her lay her own forearm alongside the dog's limb. The scene rose before him.

'Look, Father.' Her voice trembled with excitement. 'Hector has a thumb like me.'

'Nonsense, child,' but he knelt beside her to see with her eyes. The dog's dewclaw, shrunk and powerless, did indeed occupy the place of a human thumb.

'Father, why would God make Hector with a thumb he has no need of?'

Before he could answer, her mind raced on. Running her hand up from the hound's claws, tracing the bones beneath the fur, she whispered, 'Fingers. But they are under the skin. Only the tips are parted.'

Eyes wide in wonder, she then turned to the animal's back leg, tucked beneath him, feeling round the hock, its lateral protrusions and its bony point attached to the upper part by thick tendon. Ripping off the stocking from her sound leg she cradled the heel.

'See, Father. Hector's hock is the same as my heel. He's just like us but with different measurements.'

He remembered feeling both intrigued and troubled as he answered, 'Hector has flesh and bones, Blackbird, suited to his purpose. If some resemble ours, that is God's work but only we are made in His image.'

'But what of the thumb, Father? How is that suited to his purpose? Isn't it rather a detriment, since it can become entangled with other things and tear?'

'Enough, child. Come, sing to me.' He had resolved that the next night they would read the first book of Genesis and wonder together at the pattern of God's creation.

And they did. But when they came to the making of Eve, again he had noted the signs of concentration. Her brow furrowed. She began her enquiry with playful logic.

Were all female animals made from male ribs?

No, Blackbird, when God made them, he made them male and female.

Why, then, in making Man, did God not anticipate Adam's wish for a mate and create Eve at the same time? Surely, if he made only Adam, there would be no race of mankind.

God created man and later woman to be his helpmate.

Is the cow the bull's helpmate, and the mare the stallion's?

Do not question too closely. Let us continue.

But she was not to be silenced.

Father, if Adam gave up a rib to make Eve, why are not all men born with one rib less?

And she had laughingly run her hands down each side of his shirt, quietly counting.

See, there are twelve on each side. And you are a son of Adam.

He had smiled. The lightness of her fingers reminded him of Eleanor. She had so much of her mother in her. Taking her hands from his sides, he had said gently, 'Let's not question God's work too closely. There are sacred mysteries we can only wonder at.'

Yes, he had felt pride in her hunger for knowledge but was troubled when he saw her haunting the kitchen, taking and carefully cleaning left-over bones, once reassembling the carcass of a goose, measuring the wing and stretching out her own arm thoughtfully. Later she would sharpen a quill and, in a small notebook stitched from scraps of vellum, make meticulous drawings of these skeletons, the parts of which she would number and label fingers, heel, forearm, collar, toes.

Once she had held out to him two piles of bones. 'Father, feel how much lighter is the goose carcass than the hare's, though they are of much the same size. Do you think the bird's bones grew lighter because it had to fly?'

His piety had been oddly disturbed.

'They were made by God, Blackbird, some to fly, some to run and some to go like the serpent on their bellies all the days of their life. Do not question too closely,' was all he could say.

As Voted for by Students

As Voted for by Students
by *AJ Shelton*

And the stage expands, dusty curtains to velvet drapes
And boxes and crowds, and the heat from the lights
Follow the dancer as she pirouettes
But she does not try the grand jeté and pauses on the brink
Slightly breathless and the theatre exhales; dust motes
Twirling in sunlight beams from tears in covered windows.
Then she picks up the posters for the under-6's Christmas performance
Of Sleeping Beauty

The thud of a drum marches him down the corridor
Straight-backed , with the drill commands in his ears. He checks his moustache,
Wax shining on the grey bristles, before entering the mess hall.
You could cut yourself on his trouser crease.
But he doesn't recognise all the old people inside being waited on
With military efficiency by staff who notice him standing there in his slippers and shuffle him back to his room
His walking stick tapping an uncertain beat.

While he presents to an enraptured classroom, enthused for history,
hanging on his words, the students make balls from paper
torn from the edges of the worksheets to flick at their peers,
bent over mobiles or slouching half dozing. For a moment he recalls
the assembly and wonders where the certificate went.
Somewhere in the quiet loft, in a box, in faded newspaper wrapping
Most Inspirational Teacher
As Voted For By Students

Our Virtual Friends

In the middle of lockdown 2020, Wednesday Writers began to hold open mics on Zoom, just amongst ourselves. It soon dawned on us that actually, there was nothing to stop anyone, from anywhere in the world, joining in. We started inviting some of our Twitter mutuals, and before long we had a monthly-ish online event, pulling in around 50 people each time and attracting brilliant performers from Ireland, Italy, India, and even countries that don't begin with an "I".

All this continued throughout 2021 – we now get called '...one of the best open mics around'. It has even led to the setting up of a breakaway group, Todmorden Writers' Collective, who focus on organising events and opportunities for underrepresented writers. Find us on Twitter @ItsTheTWC.

The inclusive atmosphere and global reach of the Zoom open mics has been one of the bright spots in the difficult days of Covid, and lifted us up when things were bleakest. Our growing open mic 'fam' has become really important to us, and we're planning hybrid in-person/Zoom events for 2022. So we wanted to say thanks, by including in this anthology a few contributions from people who, but for the pandemic, we might never have had the chance to work with.

Zoë and Theresa
TWC
November 2021

Contents

The Tulip
by Marty Temkin

I am a child of three
with a runny nose.
I tug at a sleeve of my mother's fancy coat. Her matching
fur muff. I am cold and want to go home.
I'm hungry. My feet are wet.
The figure skates so tight,
my toes burn.

My mother is someplace else.

C'mon, dance with me, she says.
She twirls me. Like a mother duck, she shields me. I am
under the wing of her cashmere scarf.
She's skating to a medieval melody. I hear generations of
mothers comforting whining daughters.
I am grateful. I am graceful.
I won't fall.

This is a mother I haven't met before.

She glides in a figure eight. Her skates swish and swirl.
She is a mere girl.

We are petals on the same tulip,
my young mother and me.
We bend, we gently unravel from all worldly woes in the
crisp February air.
Silent snowflakes, we
curtsy on the pond.

Cave Painting
by Lindy Newns

A woman scrawled
the hunt in ochre
left charcoaled
handprints on the walls
drew that man
with beak of bird
sprawled on the earth
entranced or dead
a bull an aurochs
men with spears
horses with full
rounded bellies.

I must unlearn
what I have learned
strip away layers
of words and thought
in search of that reward
which comes when
one makes sense
of what was lost
now surfacing
from layers of ash
from dreams of death
from nakedness

daubed in paint
thick with meaning

Rebel for Life
by Stephen Smythe

Tina didn't see Michael from one year to the next when he'd turn up uninvited on Christmas Day. He'd bring out-of-date chocolates wrapped in plain brown paper for the children.

He went to church on Christmas morning – he said Midnight Mass didn't count – and arrived as Tina was dishing up the nut roast. He ate two portions of vegan pudding and guzzled the good wine. Nobody unwrapped the chocolates.

Tina seated Michael next to her husband James, away from her. She could only take so much of Michael's BO blended with his car-boot-sale cologne.

He looked like he'd given up halfway through shaving, and wore stained jeans and torn t-shirts with slogans. On consecutive years he had 'Rebel for Life' emblazoned across his chest and underneath in smaller lettering, 'Barnsley 10K'.

Each year, Tina knew less and less about Michael: whether he'd moved out from his parents, if he'd met anybody suitable, or if he still worked in toxic chemicals. When she'd ask him, he'd answer, 'Can't complain,' and change the subject.

Michael insisted on organising the Christmas quiz. He'd ask, 'According to the book of Deuteronomy how old was Moses when he died?' The children pleaded for questions about Rudolph.

Once, Tina thought Michael intentionally brushed against her at the fridge.

On Christmas night in bed, tipsy and exhausted, and with James snoring and farting, Tina could never recall as the years went by whether she'd met Michael through her husband, or one of her ex-boyfriends.

Non-Compliant

by Dee Allen.

America's the one country I know
That had been consistent,
Number one at being

Non-compliant

To agreements on the environment—
At those international shindigs with
All the countries in attendance,
Count on America's reps
To start heading
For the nearest exit door.

Non-compliant

To the call to solve
The problem of global
Climate change.
Cut the use of ancient
Dinosaur bones that make our cars go?
"Unrealistic! Let those other countries cut theirs!"

Non-compliant

To the needs of sky and earth—
Atmosphere's so full
Of greenhouse gases,
The lower world feels
Like we're living in a blast furnace.
Everything burns, everyone wilts.

Non-compliant, unwilling

To work to shift this escalating crisis—
Bringer of violent wind, sudden wildfires,
Smoky orange sky, drought, flood waters,
Loss of forests,
Loss of animal species,
Biodiversity out the door—

Non-compliant, only willing

To concentrate on the bottom line—
All petrol companies, supporting
Banks, Federal Reserve, politicians
Care about is profit. On the move to great
Capital gains, laying miles of pipe under
Land [no matter whose], crude oil to flow between
nations—

Non-compliant, slowly killing

Our planet's health—
Wind farms, electric cars,
More biodiesel vans and trucks,
More solar panels on buildings
Point to ways
Sparing us from oblivion—

Boleyn

by Lynn Walton

*(Written by Anne's best friend who considerately planned a
girly get-together on the evening before Anne was executed)*

it'll be fine you'll hardly feel a thing
let's have a last girls' night in
everyone round to your tower
you'll look great lose weight
we'll go through your outfits and check
for something stylish with a low neck
a Victoria Beckham would turn heads
get the respect of your subjects
and red would so go with the blood
black accessories so everyone
will appreciate how you create
a state occasion
let's take selfies shake this fake news
you couldn't have time for adultery, incest AND conspiracy
not with all your royal responsibility
not to mention the creation of the reformation
can you get a lipstick to match your bloodgroup
that would be so on trend on facebook
more likes than the entire Tudor timeline
front cover of Hello
peasants can vote for their favourite Boleyn moment
be seen more than Jane Seymour
just cos you had a Tudor for a suitor
who turned out to be a serial seducer
was so not your fault
let's do tequila shots

you've no worries about headaches or hangovers
we could sleep over or get an uber home
what about face masks
waxing eyebrows
cucumber eyepacks
a YouTube tutorial on red stained hairstyles
something that won't fall out when it falls off
firm hold hairspray
mustn't let a strand stray
we'll whiten your teeth
keep that regal smile on your face
secure your place on the history syllabus
there'll be media exposure
photographers getting closer
you don't want gross odours
get a 24 hour deodorant with spices and herbs
I'd put it on now or you won't get your money's worth
sweat stains are so last season's Plantagenet queens
shall I get Prosecco and Ferrero Rocher
or something posher
wild boar hors d'oeuvres
porpoise nibbles conga eel curried veal
Jamie's fifteen minute swan tagine
is to die for
have you got Now 1536
it's got top lute tunes with a virginal twist
they say you're having a French executioner
OMG is he a looker have you found him online
I'm sure he'll be gentle as it's your first time
and you've only got a little neck
you'll go viral I am well jel
post on twitter #don't lose your head
update your profile
an alive then beheaded
hope you've learnt your lesson

10 second makeover edition
this will be a media sensation decapitation
have you got the executioners number in your phone
if you don't mind me texting him when you're done

Innocent Until Proven Guilty
by Pauline Omoboye

Three black youths, one the owner of a car
Followed by police
They won't get far
Although quite innocent
And still not charged
The street is a courtroom
The judge is the sarge

I was a witness I naturally shook
My mind in turmoil
My body deep in shock
I was a witness
I naturally shook
But all I could do was stand and look

Total provocation is what I saw
Vicious manhandling and plenty more
Shouting abuse – unnecessary force
Police against black – naturally, of course

Innocent bystanders shout in disgust
Male onlookers join in the fuss
All quite reluctant, we view the situation
Everybody anxious, we shake in desperation

I was a witness
I tell no lies
Seeing is believing
I heard the cries...
...I saw the young police man, handcuffs in hand
Beating the head of an innocent man
I heard the YELL, I could almost feel the pain
As the weapon was lowered, again and again

I was a witness
A witness I was
I saw the injustice take part in the Moss
I saw the youths bundled in the van
Dragged down the street like dogs – not men
The sorrow I feel...
The hurt so real...

But only a witness what am I to do
But tell you the story so sad and true.

and so the perfect bird sang
by John Taylor

a troubling song
a song that arched from its trembling beak
singing from a silver birch in a thinning wood
a tall tree dipping and swaying
with its troupe of graceful whisperers
miming the first elegant steps
a ritual dance towards the season's end

all through that day it sang
into a dying sun settling quiet into dusk
and in the valley below
the yellowed fields and grey houses of stone
creep towards bronze
silent into flame
bathed in the golden echoes of the tireless bird

on into the night it sang
until
in the grip of the growing dark
the trembling bird fell
long and hard
lay cold and still

and when the morning struck again
fingering the dawn shadows where the dying bird had bled
it uncovered the pearled droplets of its frozen notes
staining the campion leaves black not red
and still the day came slowly
a pale light emptying the fields
spreading the slow white grief of loss

then out of a sudden fire of dawn
another voice rose in a wooded cleft
rising far off from a stunted elm
not yet felled by blight
summoning a chorus of enchantment
 a charm that clung to the leaves
rippling through the mourning trees

and in the valley bottom
fires were lit
chimneys smoked
and tired people
roused
set out for work

The Contributors
In alphabetical order

Dee Allen.

African-Italian performance poet based in Oakland, California U.S.A. Active on creative writing & Spoken Word since the early 1990s. Author of 7 books—*Boneyard, Unwritten Law, Stormwater, Skeletal Black* [all from POOR Press], *Elohi Unitsi* [Conviction 2 Change Publishing] and coming in February 2022, *Rusty Gallows* [Vagabond Books] and *Plans* [Nomadic Press]—and 43 anthology appearances under his figurative belt so far.

Lindy Newns

Lindy Newns is an award-winning playwright. She has been writing poetry for a few years and has had a number of her poems published. She sometimes struggles to remember that it is the process that matters, not winning prizes, but is getting better at this with age.

Pauline Omoboye

She considers her words quite lyrical
She gives an insight into her life
Telling stories of many injustices
Her words often cut like a knife
So cast your eyes over her writing
Sit back relax and take heed
And I hope that you will agree with me
Her words are a really good read.

Stephen Smythe

Stephen Smythe is a Mancunian writer of short fiction and poetry. In the past five years he completed an MA in Creative Writing at Salford University and reached the shortlist of the Bridport Prize (Flash Fiction category). He was also longlisted for the Bath Flash Fiction Award, finished second in the Bangor FORTY WORDS competition and third in the Strands International Flash Fiction Competition. He has also had several poems published online.

Marty Temkin

Marty Temkin (she/her) is a graduate of Boston University. She is an award-winning copywriter and has been coined an 'accidental poet'. She is currently working on her first chapbook and novel. Her work has appeared in several venues including NPR (National Public Radio in the US). She lives in New York City.

John Taylor

John likes D minor.
Compulsive writer without any idea from whence the words come. Old (and old-fashioned) and un-mellowed. Amused by his own despair.

Lynn Walton

Lynn Walton gets lots of inspiration from real events but loves looking at them from different angles and fusing things together that don't necessarily belong with each other.

with huge thanks to
all the Zoom performers of 2021

• A.R. Salandy • Anisha Kaul • Ashley Sapp • Atlas Sariol • Cayn White • Charlotte Eichler • Clare Mulley • Cleo Asabre-Holt •Damien Donnelly • Darren J Beaney • David Villegas • Eamon Somers • Elizabeth M. Castillo • Emma Storr • Fokkina McDonnell • Fran Fernández Arce • Gaia Rajan • Gaynor Jones • Helen Heery • Ian Marriott • Jay Sandhu • Jane Burn • Jazeen Hollings • Jeremy Cantor • Jonathan Evans • Juanita Rea • Kara Knickerbocker • Katie Atkinson • Keiron Higgins • Keyana The Artist • Keysha Wall • Kitty Donnelly • Lindz McLeod • LKN Poetry • Louise Wallwein • Marion Oxley • Mark Coverdale • Matthew Freeman • Michael Burton • Michael Conley • Michael Thornton • Michelle Moloney King • Miss Airedale • Nancy • Nandi Jola • Naoise Gale • Nick Steel • Philip Cook • Rachel Bennett • Renee Agatep • Rose Drew • Sarah Dixon • Sarah Reeson • Sunita Thind • Suraj A • Susan Darlington • Teresa Ogden • Tessa Foley • The Withdrawn • Tricia DeJesus-Gutierrez • Vron McIntyre • Zebib Abraham • Zoë Collins •

and of course, the audiences!

Ignorance and Belligerence

Ignorance and Belligerence
by *Laura Barnes*

3 German Shepherds in the bathroom and you
De-toxing on the sofa to the TV's drone
Yard full of ancient filth in boxes unlabelled
Boxes of other filth warring in your head
Damages repaid with wood filler and your hands
Rubbing, rubbing and the yellow dust everywhere
Cutlery, books, our eyes, our hair
My throat layering up a pallet's worth of resentment
Oh how we raged like monster gods in the sky.

Lovers' Rock on the radio again
Sprawled in the yard a carpet of still wolves
I insisted you bought underwear as soon as possible
Every button known to woman not pressed but pounded
Until I prickled with the smells, the sights, the sounds
And we ate like two starving animals.

Like a childish mother I'd let you in
Opened my blindingly white UPVC door
Invited in the seismic gale of you
And your skunk-tidal moods
The sweat of you, the breath of dogs so grateful
They leaked an ocean of relief
And it looked like devastation.

Oh but when you left
We were as close as secret lovers
When you left
When you left
When you finally left.

The Challenge

The Challenge
by *Dave Badrick*

Pristine white. Intimidatingly opaque.
Blankly inanimate but expectant of some lexiconic
pyrotechnics
That will flash and sparkle and die away to leave an after
image
Of a whole, satisfyingly finished verse or passage.

I have words, some new like psychopomp, hagiography
and panegyric.
But their appearance should be as one;
Not in stuttering, sequential, progressive left-to-right
separateness.

What subject would fill the blankness satisfactorily,
Or entertainingly, fulfillingly, cathartically, thrillingly?
'It's spring, the birds sing.
Children fuss, on the school bus.
Lockdown lethargy lessens' …

I hope for too much.
The process, the thinking, the imagining has its own value
Can we calibrate worthwhileness? Can we measure our
pleasure?
Is a walk whilst wondering what life poses
Worth more than vicarious pixelated pleasures of Vicarage
Road?
Or the strangled chords of 'You look to me like Misty
Roses?'

What of the end product, if any?
Can the offcuts built into a birdbox be weighed against the
words in a sonnet?
And do I need to explain?
Does it matter if a verse is understood by none
Or simply, like Berkeley's tree in the quad,
only perceived by the dog?

Wednesday 7.30 approaches.
Productively pressurising or crushing of creativity?
Curiously optimistic, I continue to gaze at the pristine
page.

A Thorn in your Flesh

A Thorn in your Flesh
by *Shura Price*

William's Juliet cherished your essence,
discounted, cast aside your name;
while Robbie rolled his Scottish burr
around your red, red flower:
fine symbol to celebrate romance,
in a dance of scattered petals.

Red rose: you are my token
to her,
unspoken declaration
a promise
of something
beyond words or too hard to say.

Another William
found a sickness
in your crimson folds,
but that has all withered away;
and now
while the winter snow
is full of memories,
your thorn studded black stems
bear nothing;
a painful reminder

of a woman
who could
but would not
say I love you
until the bitter end.

It is something or nothing now.

I have cut out the dead,
diseased stems
and wait for spring;
re-growth
that brings the joy of new life;
and later in the summer heat,
your scent will haunt
my garden.

Ringside Seat

Ringside Seat
by *Steve Welsh*

'When you were a boxer, grandad, did you hurt people?'

'Boxing,' he said, 'is about hurting people.'

He'd just finished cleaning up the pub downstairs and now he sat, with me on his lap, taking a rest in the afternoon before the pub opened again at teatime. He held up his clenched right fist. I gazed at the weapon that had destroyed men. The distance between his knuckles was the same as the width of my face. I nestled deeper into his body, feeling the rough hair of his long beard scratch against my cheek.

'How many fights did you have?'

'Thirty-two in all,' he said. 'I started in the Royal Navy when I was called up in the first war. But the top brass wouldn't let me sail. They wanted me to win the boxing matches against the army. And I did.'

Not for the first time, I lifted his beard and hid my face under it and he chuckled softly. I felt safe and invisible and I could feel the slow rise and fall of his chest. His beard smelt of pipe tobacco and I breathed it deep and rested into his warmth.

A few moments passed, then I lifted his beard away from my face.

'The men you hurt,' I said, 'did you want to hurt them?'

'At first I did. I had a lot of anger and the boxing brought it out of me. It was like my fists were full of hate and I had a powerful punch. Tom the Tiger they called me, and I flattened men. And when I left the Navy and got this pub, right next to the docks, well, my reputation followed me. I still boxed in amateur rounds, you see. Come closing time downstairs, when the bar was full of smoke and men, I'd shout out, 'Come on now lads, time now please.' Most days, everyone drank up and left. But sometimes there was a young feller or two watching me from a corner of the bar, who thought they'd try their luck. You could see it in their eyes. They'd think that if they could flatten me, they'd be the better man. But they all ended up on the floor and I'd drag them out by their feet and dump them on the pavement where the regulars were all waiting and cheering.'

'And what about grandma? When did you meet her?'

'Well then, I'd just dragged this young feller out and laid him on the pavement and my mates were cheering, and I went back in to tidy up, and there she was, sitting on her own in the snug with a half pint of stout.

'You won't be chucking me out,' she said and she knocked back her stout, stood up, kissed me on the cheek and left. Well, I'd flattened many a man, but I've never been flattened by a woman.'

The door began to open. It was my grandma. Quick as a flash I hid under grandad's beard. The door opened and she paused a moment then said,

'Have you seen that grandson of ours?'

'Nope. Must be out playing.'

And I felt my grandad's soft chuckle. Grandma leant over him and I felt her warmth come towards me and she bent down and she kissed my grandad. I always knew it was Monday by the smell of the laundry and the smell of freshly ironed sheets. And now, as she kissed him, the smell of Monday and the smell of pipe tobacco gently filled my world.

'Well,' she said, 'Tell him, when you see him, that tea's nearly ready.'

She left the room, closing the door softly behind her.

I lifted my grandad's beard and rested my cheek on his shoulder.

'That was close,' I said.

'Aye, she'll be looking for you outside.'

After a few seconds I said, 'And did you go courting after that? After she kissed your cheek?'

'We did. We courted for a few months. She came to some of my boxing matches, but then she stopped coming. One night I asked her why and she looked me in the eye, took a deep breath and said "Tommy, it's either the boxing or me." Well, a good woman can see the better part of a man and right there and then I said "It's you, Grace. It always will be." And I never boxed after that.'

'But do you miss it? Do you miss the boxing?'

He lifted me off his knees, stood up and opened the cupboard behind him. He reached up to the top shelf and rummaged around, then he brought out two boxing gloves. The red leather was faded and cracked. He put the gloves on my hands and tied them round my wrists. There was so much room inside those gloves. Then he sat down on the edge of the chair and pushed out his head and lifted his chin.

'You can punch me,' he said.

Sheepish, I looked at him.

'Don't worry. I won't feel a thing. But I'll close my eyes and I'll remember my times in the ring.'

Gently I patted his cheek with my right hand. Then my left. Right, left. Right, left and I got a bit of a rhythm going and I could I hear him chuckle and purr with laughter.

An Oversized Purple Cardigan

An Oversized Purple Cardigan
by *Andy Fraser*

I found a purple cardigan in a bin liner;
a fusty, only just remembered purple cardigan
that stirred again a feeling thirty years old, when
two of us would pull the woollen wound around us
- our den, our purple cardigan, back again
after all this time. But it was never mine.

The faintest trace, the lightest taste, lingers.
Fingers in deep pockets, locking secrets and cheeks
at rest on breast, breathing buttered toast and coffee
roasted cold in purple folds. And regrets;
sorrows borrowed against future time
and the start of a heart that was not mine.

The Tattoo

The Tattoo
by *AJ Shelton*

He leaned back and sighed deeply, a soft moan escaping with his exhale. Sex. One of the best things on Earth. She sat back on her heels, swallowing as she did so, then reached for the glass on the side table and took a swig of her drink, the ice cooling her red lips. He patted the duvet next to him but she didn't get up – instead she traced her finger along his tattoo – it ran from the crease of his thigh and spiralled round and round his leg down to his ankle.

She peered closer, 'your tat is sooo weird.' She stroked it, which only succeeded in turning him on again. She rolled her blue eyes at him and went back to examining the tiny dots and swirls. 'What is it?'

'Ah.' He leaned back on the bed. It really didn't matter if she knew, 'It's a message.'

She joined him, her satin skin warm against his.

'I came back here illegally' he went on.

'Oh?'

'Not the first time. The first time, I was here for a year officially – on reconnaissance – but when I went home and found out what they were going to do to Earth, I knew I needed to come back.' He interlocked his fingers with hers, feeling every tiny point of contact – the senses were amazing. 'I couldn't come back using the proper route so I used... I don't know... the smugglers? Yes,' he said almost to himself, 'that's probably the right word. Smugglers. Anyway, they use official routes but not with the official processes so I wasn't sure if I'd arrive here actually remembering everything.' He paused for a moment but didn't add, or in the same shape, or even alive.

'So?' she prompted.

'Oh, yeah, so. I had this tattooed on before I left to remind me what the message was. And since I arrived back I've tried to tell all the key people but,' he shrugged, 'they didn't listen.'

She sat up and watched the dark ink for a while; it seemed to slowly curl under her scrutiny. The tattoo was like a parade of tiny, tiny ants marching in line – if each ant was a unique shape. Her drink-soothed brain made a connection, 'What do you mean, "do to Earth?" You speak so funny sometimes.' She laughed. He liked the sound of her laugh.

'I'm not from Earth,' he stared at her intently, then waved one hand in the air indicating no particular direction, 'I'm from out there. Light years away. My species did the analysis based on my reports and decided humans would be a "danger to intergalactic stability" in, like, a million Earth years' time. I tried to point out that my analysis of the data showed humans are more likely to have wiped themselves out, but no...'

She laughed again, less certainly. 'You're so funny. An alien? Ooooo.'

She caught his eye and just for a moment he allowed his transformation field to drop from his eyes, revealing his multi-lensed, huge, yellow sensory organs.

She froze and for a moment she looked as though she might scream. Her rapid breathing made her breasts jiggle and he found his human eyes drawn to them. For some reason this seemed to calm her.

'You're not going to kill me, are you?'

'No,' he propped himself up on his elbows, 'not me. Just my species.'

She fell silent for a moment. Then she jumped to her feet, grabbing the end of the bed to steady herself. 'Right. We have to do something.'

'I tried. No one would listen. Or rather they did, but then tended to direct me towards services for individuals with mental health issues. I tried. And now I can't go home again –

the smugglers don't do return tickets.' He watched her looking round for her clothes, which were out of sight on the other side of the bed. 'At least it's just humans they're targeting – all other lifeforms will be OK. They could have just destroyed the entire planet so it's a small positive.' He paused, 'They'll probably use a targeted vaporiser.'

She flopped down next to him again; she was too drunk to remain standing for long. He could feel her breath on his face. But he could also feel the gentle thrum through his body. He knew if he looked out of the window he wouldn't see anything, but they were there all the same. It was such a shame; he loved it here but only with the humans. Staying with just the plants and animals was going to be... well... boring.

'We have to do something,' she said.

'I think that unfortunately,' he watched as her skin began to evaporate like dust and her eyes started to bleed. She raised hands that were barely there to the exposed muscles on her face, even as they disintegrated, 'it may be too late.'

Traces

Traces
by *Hannah Godden*

A lamb wobbles across the lid of the moors,
mournful baaah stolen in the wind.
He follows prints in freezing mud,
tracking tufts of wool
on miserable clumps
of heather. Smells
like milk and sleep,
closer – closer –
he stops.
Her warm bulk
low in the grass,
fox-torn and bloody.
He tucks his knees under himself
and waits.
*

It already feels like a decade ago that she took
her coat from its hook, folded herself
inside it and stepped into cold,
bleak November. Sometimes,
you walk through the shape
of her perfume
and breathe
her in
like steam
from a hot drink.
The dog sniffs her jumper
which you clutch in your lap
and you say leave it too loudly. Apologise
to empty air.

Cramp

Cramp
by *Karla Butler*

Characters: David. Nathan. Adam. Ian. Kim. Katie.

Adam: Well it was my turn to choose a trip away, and all the activities. Something I hated to do. I'm more of a follower than a leader, I like to know what I'm doing and crack on with it. Same at work, I want to be left alone to do my job and go home. Bloody work have left me in charge of organising a trip away, for a selected few that may or may not get the sack after this day out. I trawled the Internet, and found something kind of fun to do – gorge walking and jumping in deep water, a bit of team building perhaps. Well the day came, I packed my bag for a weekend, my manager Dave came to my house and explained what was meant to happen at the weekend, which I agreed. A pay rise for me. That'll do nicely. A minibus was arranged for six of us.

Nathan was the youngest, 18, a bit of a pain in the neck, a bit of a prankster.

Kim, 46, a bit overweight, the office gossip, knows everything about everybody, except for me of course, but by god she has tried and tried to find out about me.

Ian, 62, young in spirit but lacks the motivation to work hard.

Last of the bunch is Katie, 32, very beautiful, sweet, comes from a rich background, but her parents won't give her a penny unless she proves herself.

The minibus was waiting down my street. I got on and saw everybody was accounted for.

***

Adam: Right guys, good and bad news. The bad news, our instructor is off sick, and I'll be taking you gorge walking, I have a key to a house in the Lake District, privately owned by the owner of our company. And David, our manager, is gonna be our driver. The journey should only take a few hours.. You'll be able to drop your bags off then the day will begin with gorge walking.

***

Adam: Right, we're here, drop your bags in the entrance. You can sort them out later. Leave your phones here please, as they'll get wet. Right, get on the bus.

***

Adam: We're here, guys. Just a few hours' walk. David's staying with the minibus, so we won't have to walk back to the lodge.

Kim: How much further? My back is bloody killing me. Whose idea was this anyway? I thought we'd be getting at least some waterproofs. I've had to carry my bloody heels.

Adam: Not much further. I promise. Stop complaining. It'll be all worth it in the end.

Ian: Hey, you know I can't go far. Got arthritis you see, in me legs. And this bloody water is getting deeper. Are we having to bloody swim back?

Katie: Right guys, I'm sure everything is in hand. Just a bit further, I'm sure of it. My daddy used to take me gorging every other weekend. It was such fun. But I do wonder why we haven't got any waterproofs on.

Nathan: Where are we? I need a fag or summat. This is frigging boring the shit out of me. I'm off back. Stuff you lot. Fucking job's not worth it.

Adam: Right, we're here. See that bit of a drop over there? Whoever jumps in, our manager says you won't get fired. And naked of course.

Ian: Who the hell do you think we are? 18-year-old nutters? Stop the bullshit. We're all gonna get fired anyway. You've been trying to get rid of me for years.

Katie: I'll do it, but you all must turn around while I jump. (Big splash)

Adam: Where's Katie? She should have surfaced by now. I can't find her. Has she drowned? She's not coming back up. It's starting to get dark. We need to go back.

Kim: My bloody leg has cramped up and I need a piss. How do we get back?

Ian: Where's Adam gone? I knew something was wrong. Who takes the worst bunch of misfits bloody gorge walking? I can't see a bloody thing. Has anybody got a phone or summat. What about you?

Nathan: It's in my bag at the house. I didn't want to get it wet.

Ian: We'll have to swim back. This bloody rain's making the water rise.

Nathan: I can't swim.

Kim: Well I'm not carrying you, Nathan. You're on your own. I'm off. See ya...

Ian: Well it's you and me. And Adam, when he gets back.

***

David: Is the plan in motion – do they know where you are, Adam?

Adam: No, they don't have a clue, I'll go back and play my part. I'll make some excuse up.

David: How's my daughter? Is she ok?

Adam: Yes, she's watching and following them in the dark. She knows what to do...

***

Adam: What you doing here all alone Kim? You should be with the others. Never mind, go ahead. David's waiting for you.

***

Adam: Hey guys, I've had a look. We're nearly to the van. Don't worry, everything's going to be fine.

Ian: Where the fuck have you been? Leaving us here alone. Poor Nathan can't swim.

Adam: Stay here Nathan. I'll be back for you, I promise. Ian, come with me...

***

Adam: Well what a night that was! Job done. A little bit messy, but now finally Katie is gonna soon be my wife. Foot in the door at last. Just need to stop the moaning coming from the cellar. Bloody Kim won't shut up. Katie was brilliant she was. Nathan drowns, Ian has a little accident downstream. Just one more job to sort out... might leave that for another day.

The Rescue Dog

The Rescue Dog
by *Deborah Lowe*

The stone was warm to the touch. The abbey ruins seemed to bask and shimmer as bees hummed between the nodding heads of the bright flowers that clung to the weathered walls.

She thought that the nave, wide open to the blue sky with skylarks singing overhead, transported the spirit far more than the dark enclosure of a carved and gilded roof would have. As if conjured by her thought, a scudding cloud blotted the sunlight and she felt suddenly chilled. How long had it been since she was last here? A lifetime ago; too long.

The sun dappled the floor as she wandered head down, studying the remnants of tiles still in position at foot of the walls. Some bore traces of intricate encaustic patterns and weathered glaze in rich earth tones. It was as she passed through a broken arch into a narrower space, still scanning the ground at her feet, that she saw it, a plain terracotta tile with the perfect imprint of a dog's paw.

One day centuries ago, this medieval dog had strayed across the still wet clay, a fleeting moment captured. While its numberless descendants had lived and died, this one tiny trace from that sunny day had stayed, housed among the finest carvings, fabrics and treasures that human artists and artisans could create.

She knelt and touched her fingers to the pad of the paw. Smiling she remembered Tilly, the scruffy, perpetually happy mongrel, her best friend. She pictured the endless childhood games, Tilly running after her, helter-skelter along a beach, tail whirling like a propeller. Sneaking into her room to sleep curled up on the end of her bed. That time she had got in from school and Tilly had inexplicably trotted up to her with an egg in her mouth and placed it with infinite care and delicacy in her outstretched palm.

The sudden barking came from very nearby. She looked up quickly; it was excited play-barking. Through the stone arch she could see the wide sunny expanse of grass beyond, empty. She climbed onto a stone step, looking around. Nothing. Maybe inside the cloisters? She jumped down quickly, not knowing quite why she was hurrying, following the line of elegantly carved pillars till she got to the enclosed courtyard.

She gazed around the still, silent space. An ancient fig tree stretched across one wall, its curvy leaves outstretched like hands to the sun. The air shimmered, as hot and scented as a bath. She breathed in and closed her eyes, face up to the sky, and felt the softest pressure brush against her leg, a warmth settling beside her. Eyes blinking open in surprise she looked down to see the grainy, golden sand of the cloister floor and her walking boots. But bending closer, she peered at the sandy soil by her left foot. It was pitted, marked, with four perfect paw prints.

The revelation, when it came, was like the sun coming out from behind clouds. She could have a dog now. Her own dog, nothing to stop her. Maybe offer a rescue dog a loving home. They could walk and play, explore new places together. Yes, she smiled, nodding to herself, a rescue dog.

The shutters were down on the refreshment kiosk as she headed for the exit. Her car was solitary now, marooned on the wide gravel expanse of the car park. Stowing her boots in the back, she rounded to the driver's side and stopped dead. There was something small and bright on the ground just beneath the door. She knelt and set it delicately on her outstretched palm. Whole and perfect, a pale blue speckled egg.

She was still smiling as she drove out through the gatehouse. The ruined walls became filigree silhouettes against the setting sun. The slanting rays, honey gold, illuminated a halo of fur around the small, scruffy dog as it ran in wide joyful circles on the abbey meadow.

Glenys Halliday

Thank you for the words
that put a smile on the world.

Trip to Rochdale
by *Glenys Halliday*

Due to eye ops and Covid, I've not left Toddy town
But ever optimistic, don't let it get me down.
Eighteen months was long enough, and two jabs I'm okay
So, boarding the 590 bus, I soon was on my way.
To Rochdale I was heading, of that there was no doubt
Decided I would check the new shopping centre out
First a stroll down Yorkshire Street, to see how it was
doin'
Alas the Wheatsheaf Centre's shut, was this to be my
ruin?
Going there to find a loo, I was rather shocked
To notice that the lights were on, but the entrance door
was locked.
Dashing to the other one, I got there just in time,
Put twenty pence into the lock and all was going fine
But then on my departure, I hit upon a snag
The turnstile wouldn't operate, I stood there with my bag
Toilets were isolated, so leaned over stile to see
If anyone in the corridor would come and assist me.
Well, the place it was deserted, the passage it was clear
I wondered just how long I would be imprisoned here.
If it wasn't used a lot, and the cleaner seldom came
That might not be for ages; how long must I remain?
I couldn't clamber over top, the stile was far too wide
And think of the indignity if I got stuck astride.
I then espied a little gap, could I crawl through on my
knees?

I prayed my hips would not get jammed, and just slid
through with ease
I wriggled through that tiny space, though I don't want to
brag
There was plenty room to slither out, with my shopping
bag.
I quickly dusted myself off, then scuttled down the aisle
I spied a lady rushing past, you know it's not my style
Not to speak of problems, so in helpfulness I said
Do not use these toilets, choose another one instead
Explaining my dilemma, that to exit had to crawl
She said... follow the instructions, there's a button on the
wall.

My Garden
by *Glenys Halliday*

What I want, if you will pardon
Is to acquire a plastic garden
No wriggling worms to eat the roots
No greenfly gobbling up the shoots
No dandelions, no stinging nettles
No withering leaves a-spot brown freckles
No dirty fingernails or thorns
Nor snails to flex protruding horns
No ants to bite, no wasps to sting
I'd be quite safe, not do a thing
But if it did need freshening up
Just hurl wash-up liquid from a cup
Then when it does start to rain
It would be good as new again
Although I'd never be content
Until I'd sprayed it all... with scent

The End

The Contributors
In alphabetical order

Dave Badrick often wondered if he had a creative side (other than producing elegantly crafted computer programs and business studies lectures). He finally plucked up courage to join the group. He finds writing and performing in public quite daunting but appreciates the feedback.

Laura Barnes loves to think about the best place to get potatoes and finally has a decent pair of fluffy slippers. She's often found in her studio making a mess.

Karla Butler likes to write dark, gothic horror. She also likes a good bake-off. Karla combines the two for the most entertaining, bonkers characters.

Andy Fraser recently became a doctor. No, not the useful kind. Not the kind they ask for in an emergency, though he'd give it a go, if asked. He has led the Wednesdays with an iron fist for fourteen years, so feels a coup is just round the corner.

Hannah Godden edits legislation by day and enjoys writing more creative things the rest of the time. When not editing or writing (or finding dozens of household jobs to avoid both), she can usually be found somewhere in the hills getting rained on with the dog.

Glenys Halliday passed away this year. She had been a pillar of the Todmorden community and a figurehead for the Silver Surfers. Her poems, always accessible, often hilarious, will long outlive her.

Richard Holley has managed, by hook or by crook, to get a piece of writing into every anthology. When not writing, he will be found strutting and fretting his hour upon the stage.

Deborah Lowe has been coming to the group for a few years now. She still hopes to write a proper scary ghost story one day. In the meantime she writes relentlessly cheerful stuff while she waits for the dark, gothic muse to strike.

Iain Mackness has lived in Todmorden for nearly four years and enjoys the creative atmosphere and fresh air. He has a cat called Mikey, a hectic job in radio, and also volunteers at the Hippodrome theatre. When he finds time for it, writing helps to release his inner demons.

Gina Perry has a passion for folklore and mythology. She loves exploring the stunning Calder Valley and using it to inspire her work.

Shura Price is a reluctant writer, preferring to garden and drink wine. But she loves being part of this talented and friendly group of wordsmiths, so with the occasional help of a rhyming dictionary, she keeps trying.

AJ Shelton tries to juggle writing Wednesday Writers' challenges with house renovation, caring for a menagerie of demanding animals and procrastinating over several nearly-finished novels. She dreams of winning the lottery so she can finally stop work, sit down and write to her heart's content.

Theresa Sowerby enjoys writing and free meals with food critic husband, Neil. When not indulging herself, Theresa can be found wandering the hills, muttering lines for her next poem to Captain Smidge, Chihuahua and literary critic; or hosting open mics, with co-hosts Zoë and, of course, Captain Smidge.

Steve Welsh has more time for writing, having retired from the world of advanced capitalism.

Cover Photography by Graeme Scott
Cover Design by Andy Fraser
Chapter Photography by AJ Shelton, Andy Fraser & Graeme Scott